Needs an‹

Written by Margie Burton, Cathy...

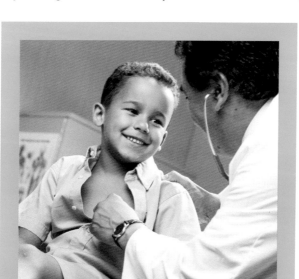

We need a house.

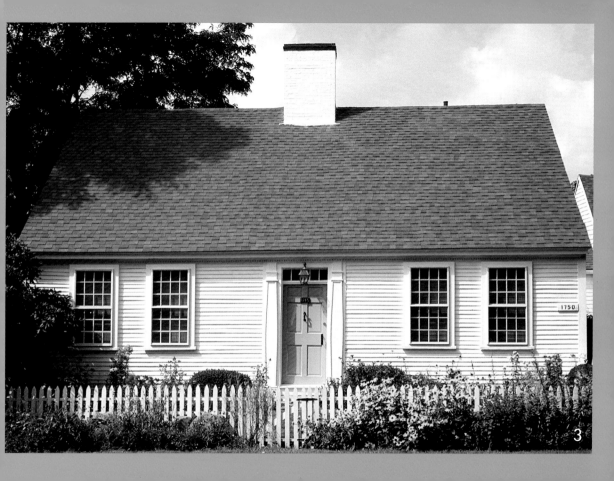

Do we need
this house?

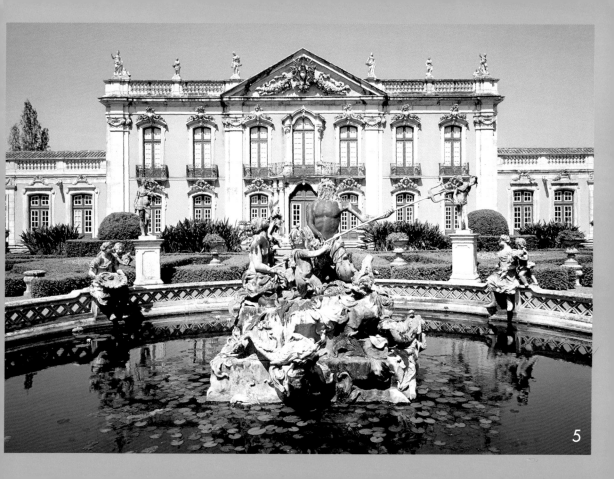

We are hungry.
We need
to eat food.

We need
to drink, too.

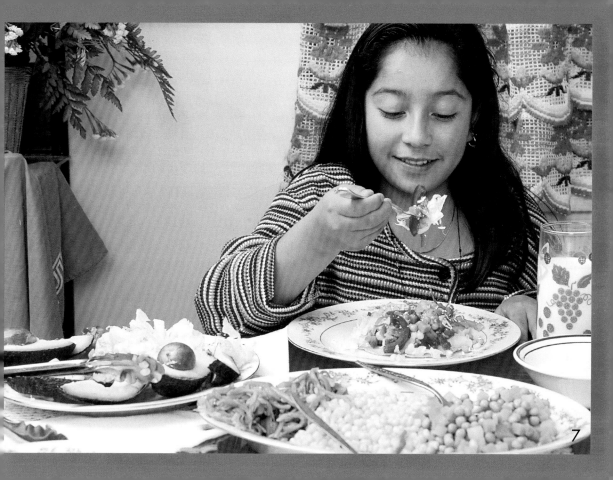

Do we need
to eat this?

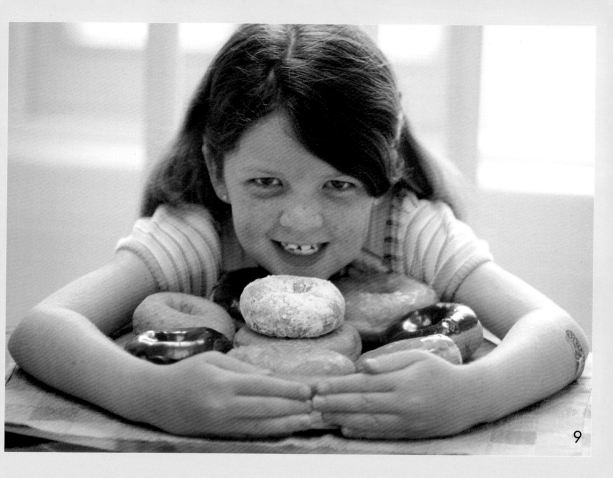

We need to play.

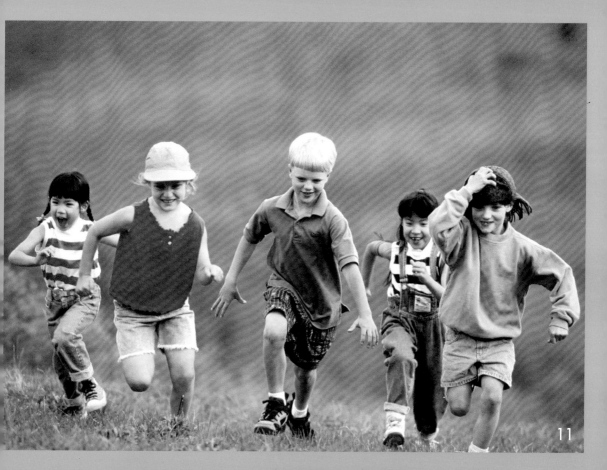

We need to sleep.

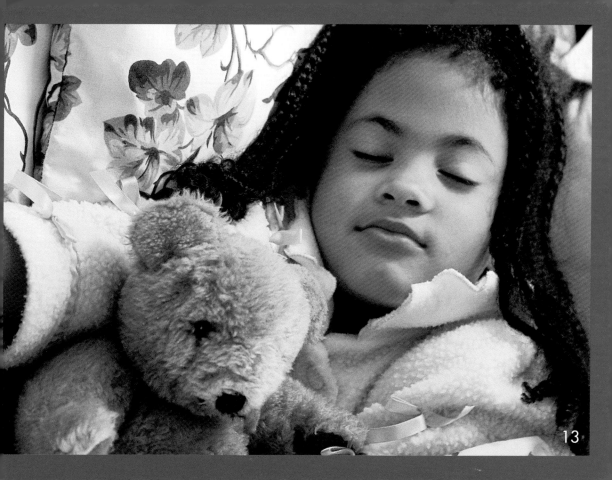

We need clothes.

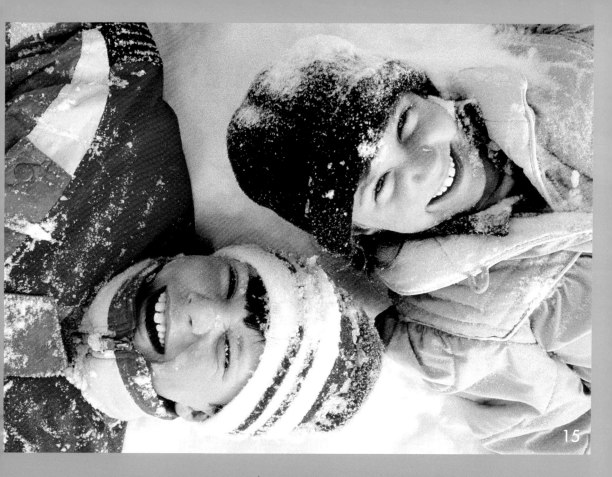

Do we need hugs?

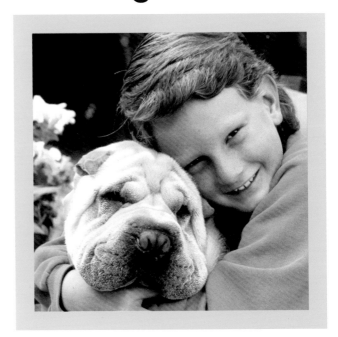